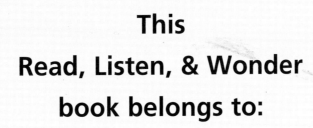

This
Read, Listen, & Wonder
book belongs to:

_____

_____

_____

**CANDLEWICK PRESS**

There are **seventeen** kinds of penguin, but the Emperor is the only one that breeds in Antarctica in midwinter. The adults arrive at their breeding areas — often more than 100 miles from the open sea — in late autumn. A few weeks later the female lays her single egg and returns to the sea, leaving the male to keep the egg warm until it hatches a couple of months later.

At first the male and female take turns caring for the chick. But soon it is big enough to be left while both parents go fishing for its food in the sea. By the time it is four months old, the young penguin's coat of down has been replaced by adult feathers. It now also sets off for the sea, where it has to start taking care of itself.

For James, John, Steve, Tim, and Tony—
and all the other dads
M. J.

For Mum and Dad,
from egg number one!
J. C.

Text copyright © 1999 by Martin Jenkins
Illustrations copyright © 1999 by Jane Chapman

First U.S. paperback edition with CD 2008

The Library of Congress has cataloged the hardcover edition as follows:

Jenkins, Martin.
The Emperor's egg / Martin Jenkins ; illustrated by Jane Chapman.
p. cm.
Summary: Describes the parental behavior of Emperor penguins, focusing on how the male keeps the egg warm until it hatches and how the parents care for the chick after it is born.
ISBN 978-0-7636-0557-5 (hardcover)
1. Emperor penguin—Behavior—Juvenile literature. 2. Parental behavior in animals—Juvenile literature.
[1. Emperor penguin—Habits and behavior. 2. Penguins—Habits and behavior. 3. Parental behavior in animals.]
I. Chapman, Jane, ill. II. Title.
QL696.S473J45  1999
598.47—dc21    98-46839

ISBN 978-0-7636-1871-1 (paperback)
ISBN 978-0-7636-3825-2 (paperback with CD)

2 4 6 8 10 9 7 5 3 1

Printed in China

This book was typeset in Humana.
The illustrations were done in acrylics.

Candlewick Press
2067 Massachusetts Avenue
Cambridge, Massachusetts 02140

visit us at www.candlewick.com

# The Emperor's Egg

Martin Jenkins

illustrated by Jane Chapman

CANDLEWICK PRESS
CAMBRIDGE, MASSACHUSETTS

Down at the very bottom of the world, there's a huge island that's almost completely covered in snow and ice. It's called Antarctica, and it's the coldest, windiest place on Earth.

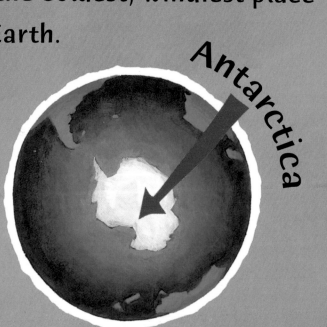

Antarctica

The weather's bad enough there in summer, but in winter it's really terrible.

It's hard to imagine anything actually living there.

But wait...
what's that shape over there?
It can't be.

# Yes!

# It's a penguin!

It's not just any old penguin either.
It's a male Emperor penguin
(the biggest penguin in the world),
and he's doing a Very Important Job.

He's taking care of his egg.

Male Emperor penguins are about 4 feet tall.

The females are a little smaller.

He didn't lay it himself, of course.

His mate did that
a few weeks ago.

But very soon
afterward
she turned around
and waddled off
to the sea.

That's where female Emperor penguins
spend most of the winter — swimming about,
getting as fat as they can
eating as much as they can,
and generally having a very nice time
(as far as you can tell)!

Emperor penguins eat mainly fish, squid,
and tiny shrimplike animals called krill.

Which leaves
the father penguin
stuck on the ice with
his egg.

Now, the most important
thing about egg-sitting is
to stop your egg from
getting cold.

Inside the egg, a penguin chick is starting to grow.

If the egg gets cold, the chick will die.

That means it has
to be kept off the ice
and out of the wind.

And what better
way to do that than
to rest it on your feet
and tuck it right up
under your tummy?

Which is just what the father penguin does.

And that's how he'll stay for two whole months, until his egg is ready to hatch.

Can you imagine it?
Standing around in the freezing cold
with an egg on your feet
for **two whole** months?

*Female Emperor penguins lay one egg in May or June,*
*which is the beginning of winter in Antarctica.*

What's more, there's nothing for
the father penguin to eat on land.

So that means two whole months
with an egg on your feet
# and no dinner!

I don't know about you

And because he's egg-sitting,
he can't go off to the sea to feed.

Or breakfast      or lunch      or snacks.

but I'd be **very, very** miserable.

Luckily, the penguins don't seem to mind
too much. They have thick feathers and lots of
fat under their skin to help keep them warm.

And when it gets really cold and
windy, they all snuggle up together
and shuffle over the ice in a great big huddle.

Most of the time, the huddle trundles along
very, very slowly.

But **sometimes,**

when the penguins get to a particularly slippery slope...

they slide down it on their tummies,
pushing themselves along
with their flippers,
always remembering
to take care of their egg —
and trying hard not to bump into each other.

Even though the males keep the egg tucked up tight under their tummies when they slide, it sometimes rolls out and breaks.

And that's how the father penguin spends the winter.

Until one day he hears a chip, chip, chip.

His egg is starting to hatch.
It takes a day or so, but finally the egg
cracks right open —

and out pops a penguin chick.

Now the father penguin
has two jobs to do.
He has to keep
the chick warm

and he has to feed it.

*The chick is only about 6 inches tall at first,*
*and much too small to keep warm by itself.*

But on what? The chick is too small to be taken off to the sea to catch food, and it can't be left behind on the ice.

Well, deep down in the father penguin's throat, there's a pouch where he makes something a little like milk. And that's what he feeds to his hungry chick.

The father penguin can make only enough of the
milky stuff to feed his chick for a couple of weeks.
But just as he's about to run out,
a dot appears on the horizon.

It gets closer
and closer
and yes!

# It's **mom!**

She starts trumpeting "hello"
and the father penguin
starts trumpeting "hello"
and the chick whistles.

The racket goes on for hours,
and it really does sound as if they're
extremely pleased to see each other.

Every adult penguin has its own special call, like a fingerprint.

Chicks have their own special whistle, too.

As soon as things have calmed down,
the mother penguin is sick — right
into her chick's mouth!

**Yuk,**

you may think.

**Yum,**

thinks the chick,

and gobbles it all down.

It's the mother's turn to take care of
the chick now, while the father sets off
to the sea for a well-earned meal of his own.

# About time, too!

# INDEX

Look up the pages to find out about all these penguin things.
Don't forget to look at both kinds of words — **this kind** and *this kind.*

MARTIN JENKINS hates cold weather and so has boundless admiration for Emperor penguin dads. As a conservation biologist, he spends most of his time writing "serious things for the World Wildlife Fund and various governments." Martin Jenkins is also the author of *Chameleons are Cool,* illustrated by Sue Shields, and *Ape,* illustrated by Vicky White.

JANE CHAPMAN says she has wanted to paint pictures of penguins ever since her honeymoon, when she visited a Scottish zoo and saw penguins waddling along on parade. She is the illustrator of *One Duck Stuck* by Phyllis Root and *One Tiny Turtle* by Nicola Davies.